How To Stop Being Selfish

The Ultimate Guide on How to be Less Selfish

Mary Peterson

Table of Contents

Chapter 1

The Paradox of Selfishness

'Don't be selfish,' is probably one of the first life lessons parents teach their children because they are all too aware of the stigma that the label selfish carries. Whether justified or not, being perceived as selfish by others can have a negative impact on your social standing. There's also a good reason for it.

Being selfish in our distant, prehistoric past meant jeopardizing the tribe's safety and cohesion. A crime of such gravity required proportionate punishment. If you were lucky, your friends would quickly murder you. The worst fate was expulsion from the tribe, which could only result in one of two outcomes: starvation or being eaten by a saber-toothed tiger.

While civilization has ensured that we can no longer club selfish people in broad daylight, the taboo surrounding selfishness persists. That is why you are not a good parent if your child refuses to share her toys and candy with others.

While selfishness remains an undesirable trait, the context in which we evaluate it has shifted dramatically. Unlike in the past, when there was no concept of individual goals, most of our personal goals are now zero-sum in nature. One person's gain is another person's loss, whether it's material success or social status, even if it's anonymous individuals competing against each other.

In other words, our success in the real world is contingent on being selfish, at least in the broad sense of only thinking about ourselves. How do we reconcile this reality with what our elders teach us about not being self-centered? This contradiction is not amusing. Most people struggle to balance the two sides, resulting in a split within themselves and an ever-present sense of guilt.

This conflict is most likely caused by the way we are taught to think about selfishness. The admonition not to be selfish is often used to suppress our spontaneity and prevent us from pursuing our own desires, especially when we are children. We've learned as adults that it's not the expression of our uniqueness, but the suppression of it, that makes us acceptable to others. Being selfless, then, is a price we must pay in order to be accepted into the groups of our choice.

Genuine unselfishness, on the other hand, is extremely difficult to achieve because it is contingent on you like the recipient of your generosity. However, because liking cannot be commanded, we end up performing unselfishness. This 'pretend' selflessness not only causes inner turmoil but also leads to a fundamental 'lack of fondness,' both for others and for ourselves.

Low self-esteem, a basic sense of low self-worth, and a constant stream of self-criticism are the most common symptoms of this lack of inner liking. We are our own slave drivers, constantly berating ourselves for failing to meet the expectations of those around us. Even our leisure time is not immune to this onslaught of negativity, as feelings of guilt for enjoying ourselves keep us on edge.

Does this imply that selfish people do not have low self-esteem? After all, selfishness, and its extreme form, narcissism, stem from an excessive obsession with oneself. To be selfish, you have to love yourself, right? Otherwise, why would you risk being called an asshole?

It is a mistake to believe that selfishness is simply excessive self-love. It's more like greed in that you can't help but take more for yourself. This greed stems from self-hatred because you can't stand who you are and want to be someone else.

Thus, selfish behavior is characterized by heightened anxiety for oneself rather than a lack of concern for others. A selfish person is constantly grasping at more and more in a desperate attempt to get closer to their ideal version of themselves.

In other words, a selfish person does not love themselves more than others. Instead, they love themselves far too little. The unconscious lack of love manifests as a lack of concern for others, a condition known as, you guessed it, selfishness.

But if I don't like who I am, why should I be cruel to others? Love is not a reaction to something outside of oneself. Rather, it is a pre-existing ability motivated by a genuine desire to see its object happy and flourishing.

So, when you hold your lover close or look at your sleeping child, the flood of emotions is not caused by you, but rather by an existing readiness that is awakened by the focus of your affection. And now comes the real question: if love is an inborn ability, how can it possibly exclude our own self?

If a person has this readiness toward himself, he also has it toward others; if he can only love others, he cannot love at all. Our feelings and attitudes are directed not only at others but also at ourselves. This means that our attitudes toward others and ourselves are not contradictory but rather run concurrently. Love for others and love for oneself are not mutually exclusive.

This lack of readiness to love is what we see and condemn as selfish behavior. Unbeknownst to us, the selfish individual has lost the ability to love herself.

This means that our parents', teachers', and society's admonitions to be selfless may be doing more harm than good. We cannot genuinely care for others while denying ourselves the same care because we are as much a part of the world as the object of our kindness. Self-denial can never be a breeding ground for generosity.

This is probably why a self-assured person is rarely selfish. When someone is comfortable in their own skin, they have a strong foundation from which to reach out and connect with others. An insecure person, on the other hand, is focused inward, desperately attempting to overcome her insecurity. And it is here that the seeds of selfishness are planted.

Unselfishness is thus a state attained indirectly, rather than directly, by becoming the type of person who is incapable of being selfish. If you want to be a kind and selfless person, you must first become secure in yourself and learn to love yourself. This is not the Instagram narcissist's phony love, but genuine comfort in your own skin. To do so, you must first begin to treat yourself with kindness.

Treat yourself as if you are in charge of someone. Genuine feelings of generosity and kindness for others can only come from a place of confidence in oneself. So, if you want to help others, you must first fulfill your own potential. Be wary of those who refuse to accept responsibility for themselves but wish to change the world.

So, instead of being a jerk, be selfish for a while. By becoming the best version of yourself, you can lay a solid foundation for your self-worth. Individuals who find a sense of accomplishment by dedicating themselves to the service of others are few and far between. What about the rest of us? We can help others only if we first take care of ourselves.

Chapter 2

The Effects of Selfishness on Relationships

Being in love is a wonderful feeling, and you're all set to be the best lover ever while also having a good time. However, love necessitates some learning and compromise. If you've been used to doing things your way for a long time, or if you haven't dated in a long time, your independent spirit may manifest as selfishness in a relationship. That, or you're just naturally self-absorbed and haven't learned to put others first.

While wanting to put your own needs first is not necessarily a bad thing, being selfish in a relationship can be devastating and hurt your partner. When a person begins to disregard their significant other's needs and treats them with a lack of compassion and concern, the relationship usually begins to deteriorate.

Signs of Being Selfish in a Relationship

You and your partner must be considerate of each other's feelings in order to have a healthy, loving, and mature relationship. When it comes to relationships, empathy and love go hand in hand, and selfish, one-sided relationships have consequences. It is critical to first recognize that you are being selfish and then work on yourself to allow the relationship to blossom.

When you put the 'I' ahead of the 'we' in an intimate relationship, you are being selfish. It's so ingrained in us to prioritize ourselves that we don't realize we're being selfish or hurtful to someone we care about.

Being the partner who says hurtful things, is inconsiderate, and selfish can eventually cause the other person to end the relationship. When you notice a lot of frequent arguments, it is a good idea to assess your position in the partnership. When you start asking yourself, "Am I selfish in my relationship?" you'll be surprised at how many minor issues arise that need to be addressed.

Selfish people aren't always aware of the impact their actions have on others, so anyone should make the selfish individual aware of what they're noticing about their actions, as well as the impact on themselves.

We've compiled a list of indicators that you're making your relationship all about you, rather than cultivating a strong, give-and-take partnership that will help your love last longer.

It's the highway if it's not your way
I'm an argumentative person by nature. And I prefer to have things done my way. It could be anything from how cutlery is arranged on the dining table to how a business presentation should be delivered. My partner frequently observes that I rarely give other people the opportunity to do things their way, or even consider that there might be another way.

People who are accustomed to doing things their way often find it difficult to collaborate or recognize that there are other options. It indicates a loss of control to them and can make them shaky. This can manifest as a selfish boyfriend or girlfriend dismissing their partner's suggestions or point of view in an intimate relationship.

Consider this. Is it always the case that when you and your partner have a disagreement, your word is the last? Do you even force your partner to forego their own happiness and abandon the argument? Do you become enraged or threaten to give your partner the silent treatment if you do not get your way?

Long-term, this behavior can cause resentment in your partner, leading to the end of the relationship. One of the signs you're selfish in a relationship is always having the last word and throwing a fit if things don't always go your way.

You believe you are always correct

Nobody likes a self-righteous bore. Even your partner, who claims to love you unconditionally, wishes you would stop. You don't know everything, no matter how well-read, educated, or traveled you are. And assuming you do is detrimental to your relationship.

Being unable to accept that they are ever wrong is a major sign of a self-absorbed person. They believe they are superior and are perplexed by anyone who believes otherwise. They will go to any length to prove that they are always correct. Does that describe you in any way?

One of the signs that you are selfish in a relationship is if you have a misplaced superiority complex. It's okay to set your ego aside and let go of your god complex every now and then. Furthermore, as they say, "To err is human."

You never take your partner's advice seriously

"Wait," you say. "What do you mean there are multiple points of view in this relationship?" Yes, because you're not in a relationship with yourself, you should recognize that your partner has thoughts, feelings, and opinions as well. And they might differ from yours.

If you constantly expect preferential treatment in your relationship because you believe you are the more important being and your opinions should be valued more, this is one of the clear signs you are selfish in a relationship. Not only that, but you're arrogantly assuming that your significant other lacks the ability to take a stand.

You might feel like it's not worth it to seek your partner's opinion at times. To you, does this seem like a good relationship? In any relationship, mutual respect is essential, and this includes respecting your partner's thoughts, opinions, points of view, and feelings.

You concentrate on 'winning' the argument

Look, I understand. It's incredibly satisfying for me to win arguments. However, a wise person once said that in relationships, you must sometimes choose between being right and being together. And if you always choose to be right, chances are you won't be together for long.

Nobody is telling you to drop every argument. But consider how far you will go to win an argument. You don't care if it causes harm to your partner. You don't think twice about pushing all of their buttons, even if you know you're triggering deep-seated trauma or old wounds.

You will go to any length to win an argument because winning is all that matters to a selfish person. Losing an argument is a sign of weakness for you, and your ego drives you to fight to feed it.

In fact, if you look closely enough, you'll notice that you actually dislike losing arguments and would rather walk away than be proven wrong. If you're asking yourself, "Am I selfish in my relationship?" This is a wonderful spot to look for an answer.

Here's a hint: Winning every argument in a relationship does not make you attractive. Or give you a charismatic personality. Okay, we'll stop now.

After a fight, it is always your partner who apologizes
The word sorry is not in your vocabulary. In fact, apologizing sounds to you like giving up and admitting you were wrong. And we all know how much you despise that!

All couples fight, but if you're looking for signs that you're selfish, you'll notice that people with selfish partners are more likely to apologize even if they're not at fault. You're always defending yourself and digging your heels in, implying that it was always, always your partner's fault.

You emotionally manipulate them to believe they are always wrong, find it extremely difficult to swallow your pride, and always end up blaming your partner. Sure, happy couples fight, but they reconcile and don't play blame games.

If you can't recall the last time you sincerely apologized after a fight, you're being selfish in a relationship and need to make amends.

You are constantly attempting to assert control

You adore being in command. Of your own life, as well as everyone else's, including your partner's. To you, dominance and control are synonymous with power. And you want power because it makes you feel like a winner. You're so certain that whatever you decide is the best course of action that it never occurs to you that this could be a toxic trait that destroys your relationships.

If too many people call you a control freak, and not in a nice, quirky way, this is one of the signs you are selfish in your relationship. Selfishness destroys relationships, and if you're constantly attempting to exert control over your partner and your relationship, it can quickly devolve into a messy breakup.

It's normal to want to be directed, to want your partner to do or be better. However, you must allow them to live and grow at their own pace and not take over their entire life.

Your needs are always prioritized

'I want.' was my ex-girlfriend's favorite phrase. It didn't matter what I or anyone else wanted; her needs had to be met, and her needs were what mattered. We'd get pasta even if I wanted a burger. I wanted to stay at home, but we'd go out because she wanted to. I'd want to discuss my day, but her day was always more important.

When you believe that your needs are more important than everyone else's, this is one of the signs that you are selfish in a relationship. You're convinced that no one has it as bad as you do and that your cries must be heard first, before anyone else's.

Again, this can lead to significant resentment in a marriage or relationship. Your partner may sulk in silence for a while, but eventually, they will either abandon their own needs entirely to prioritize yours, or they will simply leave the relationship.

That, my friend, is yet another strong indicator of selfishness in a relationship, as well as one of the characteristics of a self-absorbed person who makes their relationships all about them.

You frequently guilt-trip your partner
Another sign that you are selfish in a relationship is that you guilt trip your partner to ensure that your needs and desires are met. Guilt trips are an obvious manifestation of psychological manipulation and coercion. You manage to make your partner feel guilty for anything that does not go your way.

In other words, you're telling your partner that they should feel bad about themselves because things didn't go exactly as planned. And this happens whenever you are dissatisfied with the way things are.

Guilt-tripping is a terrible, passive-aggressive way to express your displeasure with a loved one. It creates spectacularly unhealthy relationships and emphasizes your selfishness in a relationship.

You are an expert at duping your partner
You certainly are! Remember how you withheld sex and sulked in cold silence until your partner caved to your demands? You actually think and practice unhealthy tactics to get them to work the way you want them to. When your partner disagrees with you on something, you ignore them until they agree.

This can deeply hurt your partner, and they may begin to harbor resentment towards you, even if they don't express it right away. Remember that accumulated bitterness and negativity are more likely to result in a painful and abrupt end to a relationship.

You are constantly competing with your partner
If your partner gets a new job or a raise, you are not happy and instead focus on how to beat him or her. Simply put, you regard them as a rival rather than a collaborator. Not only that but when you're having a difficult time at work, you expect your partner to pitch in, even if it means sacrificing their own work or priorities.

You are constantly competing with your partner, and you even expect them to make unhealthy sacrifices to help you 'win,' which is clearly one of the signs you are selfish in a relationship. There could also be some unhealthy jealousy at work.

Though it is important to be competitive in a world where the mantra is survival of the fittest,' competing against your own partner or walking all over them will only lead to bitter times ahead. It is not a good idea to compete with your partner.

You have issues with trust
You are self-centered, and you are aware of it. So, obviously, you can't rely on your partner to make you happy because you've come to believe that only you can bring happiness to yourself. In a relationship, you never give 100% of yourself, and you assume the other person will do the same. As a result, your relationships do not last long.

One of the signs of a self-absorbed person in a relationship is having major trust issues for no apparent reason. However, you should be aware that selfishness has consequences in a relationship.

You believe you are a better option for your partner
Your superiority complex leads you to believe that your partner is flawed while you are perfect. You frequently express that they are not "good enough for you." You believe you score higher on all fronts, whether it is their physical appearance or psychological factors. And where you don't, it's most likely insignificant.

This leads to another major expectation: that your partner will change themselves to be what you want, to 'improve' and meet your standards.

You contribute nothing to the relationship
You never seem to put any effort into the relationship; instead, you only complain about it not being what you 'expected'. You are unconcerned about your partner's happiness, and your plans revolve primarily around your own interests and likes.

You never compromise, and if you do, it's usually as a favor. You never try to make up after a disagreement and are still upset if your partner does not give their all to the relationship.

This can make your partner frustrated and want to end the relationship over time. And who can blame them?

In the short run, you have the freedom to be selfish, but the consequences of selfishness will eventually catch up with you.

Chapter 3

Relationships Are Ruined by Selfishness

If you recognize most of these signs of selfishness in a relationship, you need to examine yourself and make some changes in how you treat others, especially your partner.

Being selfish and putting yourself first is not always synonymous. When you're selfish, you're barely perceptive to the needs and desires of those around you, which is bad karma.

You willfully do things that you know will cause harm to others simply because you can and want to, regardless of the consequences of selfishness. You frequently take your partner for granted. But believe us when we say they won't put up with it forever.

Here are a few examples of how selfishness ruins relationships:

Your partner believes he or she is unloved or uncared for
When you're the self-absorbed partner in the relationship, you want your partner's attention as well. This will almost certainly make your spouse feel insignificant and unloved. They will be distracted, which brings us to the next point.

They begin to harbor resentment
Resentment arises as a result of your partner putting everything into the relationship but receiving little in return. They'll notice your selfish behavior and need to be right all the time, regardless of the consequences.

Your relationship's fights are becoming more frequent
When a person is unhappy in a relationship, they begin to project their dissatisfaction in the form of arguments. Because they are

dissatisfied with how you treat them, your partner will start picking fights with you more frequently.

Your partner no longer gives in to your every demand
They will no longer give in to your every whim and fancy because they are aware of your selfish behavior. This may enrage you and lead to more fights, but perhaps it's time to reflect on yourself.

They complain to you about how things aren't going well
Your partner may try to communicate with you about how they believe things aren't going well and how they are unhappy. If/when they do this, do your best to listen to them and avoid shifting blame. If you truly want your relationship to succeed, now is the time to show your partner that you care.

Your partner meets someone new
If, despite them expressing their feelings to you, you remain obstinate and continue down the road to hell, your partner may find someone who values them more than you ever did.

The relationship is ending
When your partner has had enough, they will end the relationship. Or one of your arguments may become too heated, and you decide to end the relationship due to your obvious ego issues. Whatever the reason, the relationship may end in disaster.

You're having trouble moving on
Regardless of who ended the relationship, you know the main reason was your selfishness. You can try to deny it, but it will leave a mark on your conscience. This is why, if you don't mend your ways, you may have difficulty moving on after the breakup and finding a new partner.

People can be selfish in order to protect their own self-interest. They may be afraid of doing more for others for fear of putting their own needs on hold. However, in some cases, particularly in intimate relationships, this can be a toxic trait that makes the relationship dynamic one-sided.

Prioritizing goals, respecting others' time, maintaining healthy relationship boundaries, and one's own well-being are all important considerations when building and maintaining relationships. In every relationship, platonic or romantic, partners give and take in equal measure without keeping score.

A relationship with a selfish person, on the other hand, means that they take your love and affection without reciprocating. They believe they are more needed than you are.

So, how do you alter it? Accepting that you're being selfish in a relationship is the first step, followed by a genuine commitment to change. Do not panic just yet; instead, go apologize to your partner and work on making your relationship healthy for both of you.

Chapter 4

Selflessness

Selfishness and selflessness may appear to be diametrically opposed, but they are both necessary components of our lives. Being selfish can benefit individual success, but it is critical to understand the value of selflessness in order to live a fulfilled life. Self-reflection, effort, and a willingness to make positive changes are all necessary for transitioning from selfish to selfless.

Throughout history, the concept of selfishness has had an unfortunate and frequently negative connotation. We are taught that being selfish is wrong and that we should put others ahead of ourselves. But what if there was a way to strike a balance between the two—taking care of oneself while also considering the needs of those around us?

Selfishness is defined as prioritizing one's own needs and interests over those of others. In some cases, taking time for yourself can lead to increased productivity and better mental health. In other cases, however, it can devolve into toxic self-centeredness, with negative consequences for both the individual and society as a whole.

Motives for selfish behavior can range from simply wanting more resources for oneself, such as money or recognition, to feeling entitled or superior, or even viewing others as objects rather than individuals with unique needs. Whatever the motivation, it is critical to be aware of these underlying influences in order to avoid harmful or destructive actions.

Being selfish has some advantages: it can provide a sense of independence and autonomy; it can provide a sense of control; it can result in higher levels of productivity; and it can even result in better decision-making by allowing you to look at issues objectively without getting caught up in emotions or biases.

However, it has several potential drawbacks, including increased stress due to a lack of support from others; decreased collaboration, which leads to limited project progress; feelings of entitlement, which leads to disrespecting personal boundaries set by others; and, ultimately, isolation from loved ones due to a lack of compassion.

Identifying when our actions become too self-centered is critical to preventing them from having a negative impact on our lives. We must learn to recognize when we are crossing others' boundaries or engaging in behavior that benefits only ourselves without considering the impact on those around us.

It's also important not to think of selflessness as an all-or-nothing proposition; sometimes we need a balanced approach in which we take care of both our own needs and the needs of those around us. We can make the world a better place for everyone if we understand how our actions affect others. Transitioning from selfishness to healthy selflessness will benefit both ourselves and society as a whole.

Misconceptions about selflessness

Selflessness is more than meets the eye. Contrary to popular belief, being selfless does not require us to sacrifice our own needs and desires in order to benefit others. It entails striking a healthy balance between the two, pushing us to discover new aspects of ourselves that may have lain dormant until now. Furthermore, it does not necessitate much physical effort; rather, it can be as simple as donating money or volunteering time for charity work, which anyone can do.

Furthermore, contrary to popular belief, anyone can practice selflessness regardless of their intentions or motivations. The important thing is that we use our privilege responsibly and recognize when others require help so that we can assist them without expecting anything in return. We can become better versions of ourselves while also helping those around us become better, by understanding this concept and actively working to achieve a balance between our wants and the needs of those around us!

From self-centered to selfless

Being selfish can benefit individual success, but understanding the value of selflessness is essential for living a fulfilled life. Making the transition from selfishness to selflessness is not always easy, but it is possible with some effort and understanding.

The first step in making this transition is to recognize when one's actions become overly focused on one's own needs and desires rather than those of others. It is critical to consider how your decisions affect those around you and to strive for a balance between what you want and what others require. Empathy and compassion are critical in shifting from selfish to selfless behavior. It is critical to put yourself in the shoes of others and acknowledge that everyone has different needs and perspectives.

Finding ways to give back to your community or society as a whole is also part of practicing healthy selflessness. Simple actions such as volunteering for local charities or donating money can help ease the transition. Taking time out of your day to check in on family members or friends who may need assistance or advice can also help to smooth the transition from selfishness to selflessness.

Finally, when making the transition from selfish to selfless, we must be mindful of how our actions affect those around us. There will always be times when we require something for ourselves, but it is critical that we remember that there are others who require our help as well. Readers can make significant progress in making the journey from selfishness to selfless living easier and more rewarding by keeping these considerations in mind while striving for a balance between what we want and what others need. It is critical to follow these step-by-step guidelines to transition from selfishness to selflessness:

Consider your actions

Take the time to evaluate your behavior honestly and identify instances where you have prioritized your own needs over the needs of others. Recognize that self-centeredness can harm relationships and impede personal growth.

For example, if you frequently spend your free time pursuing your own interests while ignoring the needs of your loved ones, consider how this behavior may be affecting your relationships. Consider the significance of finding ways to prioritize the well-being of others as well as your own.

Empathy should be practiced

Empathy is referred to as the ability to understand and share the feelings of others. Put yourself in someone else's shoes and try to see things from their perspective or viewpoint. Strive to be compassionate and understanding and consider how your actions will affect others.

For example, if a friend is going through a difficult time, make an effort to listen attentively and offer support rather than focusing solely on your own concerns. With this shift in perspective, you can connect on a deeper level and offer genuine empathy.

Actively listening

Being selfless requires you to actively listen to others. Pay attention to what others are saying without interrupting or forming an immediate response. Validate their experiences and show genuine interest in their thoughts and feelings.

For example, when conversing, practice being completely present. Avoid the temptation to keep bringing the conversation back to yourself. Instead, actively listen to the other person's words and emotions, creating a trusting and understanding environment.

Develop a sense of gratitude

Gratitude assists in shifting one's focus away from oneself and toward the positive aspects of life and the contributions of others. Take the time to thank and appreciate those around you for their efforts and kindness. Gratitude can help to strengthen relationships and foster a sense of interconnectedness.

Make it a habit, for example, to express gratitude for small acts of kindness you receive. Thank someone for their assistance or recognize the positive influence they have had on your life. You not only uplift others, but you also cultivate a grateful and selfless mindset.

In small ways, practice selflessness

It is critical to follow these steps in order to truly transform a selfish act into a selfless act. Consider the following example:

Consider yourself in a crowded coffee shop, waiting in line for your favorite latte. As you approach the counter, you notice a person behind you who appears to be hurried and stressed. In this situation, ordering your drink without considering the person behind you would be selfish.

This selfish act, however, can be easily transformed into a selfless one. Instead of placing your order right away, step aside and give the person in front of you the opportunity to do so. This simple act of kindness demonstrates empathy and consideration for another person's time and needs. It may appear insignificant, but it can have a significant impact on both you and the other person.

Avoid seeking approval

Avoiding the constant need for validation is another example of transforming a selfish act into a selfless one. Consider the following scenario:

Assume you're working on a team project and you've worked hard to come up with an idea. It would be a selfish act to constantly seek validation and praise from your teammates, expecting them to recognize your contributions without taking into account their own ideas and efforts.

Focus on collaboration and valuing the contributions of others to transform this selfish act into a selfless one. Rather than seeking approval, actively listen to your teammates' ideas, give credit where credit is due, and foster a supportive and inclusive environment. This fosters a sense of teamwork and allows everyone's contributions to shine, not just your own.

Learn to compromise
Compromise is essential for becoming more selfless. Here's an illustration:
Assume you and a friend are choosing a movie to watch together. A selfish act would be to insist on watching your favorite movie regardless of your friend's preferences. This may cause conflict and imbalance in the relationship.

To turn this selfish act into a selfless one, be willing to compromise and look for a movie that both of you will enjoy. Consider your friend's preferences and be willing to let go of your own desires. This demonstrates a selfless approach in which you prioritize the other person's happiness and satisfaction, fostering a healthier and more balanced relationship.

Provide feedback and learn from it
It is critical to actively seek feedback from trusted individuals in your life in order to truly transform from a selfish act to a selfless act. By being open to other people's perspectives, you can gain valuable insights and identify areas for improvement. Pay close attention to their constructive criticism and use it as a springboard for self-reflection and growth.

Remember that feedback is a gift that allows us to see ourselves in a new light. Accept it with an open mind and a desire to learn. Each piece of input, whether it is feedback on your behavior, actions, or choices, provides an opportunity for self-improvement.

Surround yourself with people who genuinely care about your well-being and are invested in your personal growth when seeking feedback. These individuals can be friends, family members, mentors, or trusted coworkers. Their perspectives can help you gain a better understanding of how your actions affect others and guide you toward becoming more selfless.

Be persistent and patient
It takes time to transition from a selfish act to a selfless act. True selflessness takes time, effort, and dedication to cultivate. Be gentle with yourself as you embark on this journey of personal development.

Recognize that change is a process that may include setbacks along the way. Accept these difficulties as opportunities for growth and perseverance. Remember that every small step toward selflessness is a step forward.

Maintain your commitment to becoming more selfless, even when faced with obstacles or temptations to revert to selfish behavior. Reflecting on your actions, practicing empathy, actively listening, cultivating gratitude, and engaging in selfless acts in your daily life are all steps you should take on a regular basis.

In times of doubt or impatience, remind yourself of the benefits of selflessness on your relationships and overall well-being. With patience and perseverance, you will see yourself transform as selflessness becomes second nature.

Chapter 5

The Empathy Effect

In recent years, the process of restorative justice' has become increasingly popular as a means of dealing with crime. Offenders are brought face to face with the victims of their crimes as part of the process to hear how they have suffered as a result. The goal of this meeting is to bring healing to both the victim and the offender. The victim overcomes their rage by showing some understanding and forgiveness to the offender, and the offender empathizes with the victim, realizing the true meaning of their crimes. This procedure has an impact on people's lives. Victims are able to move on because they are no longer burdened by hatred; offenders have a broader perspective and are less likely to re-offend. Offenders may meet victims of similar crimes rather than their specific victims. However, this results in a new awareness and new behavioral patterns.

This demonstrates the incredible power of empathy. All crime and cruelty are, to a large extent, the result of a lack of empathy. It is a lack of empathy that leads to someone attacking or oppressing others. Warfare and conflict are made possible by a lack of empathy for another tribe or country. Oppression and inequality are made possible by a lack of empathy for other ethnic groups, social classes, or castes.

Empathy is the ability to 'feel with' another person, to identify with them, and to understand what they are going through. It is sometimes referred to as the ability to ' read' other people's emotions or to imagine what they are feeling by 'putting yourself in their shoes.' In other words, empathy is considered a cognitive ability, similar to the ability to imagine future scenarios or solve problems based on prior experience. However, empathy, in my opinion, is more than this. It is the ability to enter another person's mind space and make a psychic and emotional connection with them. When we feel genuine empathy or compassion, our identity merges with that of another person. The separation between you and the other person dissolves. Your self-boundary' dissolves, and in some ways, or to some extent, you become them.

If you are in this state of connection with another person, it is impossible to treat them poorly, except inadvertently. You are repulsed by their suffering in the same way that you are repulsed by your own. In fact, you have a strong desire to alleviate their suffering and help them grow.

Empathy has significant psychological benefits for us as well. According to research, empathic people are more satisfied with their lives and have better relationships. Some scientists used to believe that humans are inherently selfish and individualistic, but new research shows that empathy, not selfishness, is 'hard-wired' into us. Animals frequently show empathy for one another, even between species, and this manifests itself in random acts of kindness. Animals frequently form alliances with members of unrelated species...There have even been reports of animals from one species adopting those from another. Within their own species, animals frequently share food to ensure that weaker members of their group are fed, even if it means sacrificing their own food.

According to research, women are generally more empathic than men. Women, for example, have been shown in studies to be significantly better at reading people's emotions simply by looking at them. According to other research, women's friendships are typically founded on mutual assistance and problem-solving, whereas men typically form friendships based on shared interests such as sports and hobbies. Men and women have different speaking styles, according to research. Women's conversations tend to last longer due to their use of more 'back channel support' gestures such as nodding, smiling, and other nonverbal cues. If they disagree, they tend to express themselves indirectly rather than directly, which helps to avoid confrontation. Men, on the other hand, are more direct and opinionated. They use more imperatives and 'talk over' more often.

Men spend more time demonstrating their knowledge, skill, and status through language. This makes sense: after all, the vast majority of ' man's inhumanity' throughout history has been caused by man. Men have orchestrated and fought almost all wars, and most social oppression has been inflicted by high-status men seeking to protect and increase their power and wealth.

This is also consistent with women's roles as mothers. Because of the need for a strong emotional connection with children, their nurturing role undoubtedly encourages empathy. At the very least, this emotional bond would have made it more difficult for them to lose their ability to empathize.

In the same way that a lack of empathy allows cruelty and oppression to occur, the presence of empathy heals conflict. The greater the spread of empathy - from victims to offenders, from one ethnic group to another, from nation to nation, and religion to religion - the less brutal and more harmonious the world will become.

Perhaps most importantly, as Restorative Justice demonstrates, empathy can be fostered to some extent. When people are brought together in a neutral setting with an open, trusting attitude, empathy emerges naturally. Distinctions of ethnicity, religion, and other superficial 'identity badges' fade, as do feelings of resentment and rage derived from past events. The same could be said of nature: when humans spend time in natural settings, relaxing in their stillness and space, a bond naturally forms.

And it is this bond that is undeniably our true nature. Empathy demonstrates that the concept of separateness is illusory. Empathy is simply the experience of our true connectedness, the exchange of feelings via the channel of shared consciousness that connects all living and nonliving things.

Consider someone you care about and be aware of the warm feeling that arises within you. Hold on to that warm sensation and allow it to spread throughout your body, including any areas of discomfort. Allow it to enter your mind as well, so you can feel empathy and compassion for your own thoughts, even the negative ones. Consider all of the people in the rooms or buildings around you, and imagine the warm glow of compassion leaving your body and spreading to them. Consider all the people in your city, on the streets and in the buildings, and extend the warm feeling to them as well. Thinking of all the people in this country, in cities and in the countryside, and spreading the feeling to them as well. Then broaden it to include all people on the planet, millions of people in various countries. Feel the warmth of compassion radiating from your being out into the world and into the space above you, rising up into the sky and the entire universe.

How to Develop Empathy

Use your imagination to imagine how the world appears to other people. Consider how other people's situations affect them and how their experiences shape their perceptions.

Give others your full attention when speaking with them. Don't think about anything else, don't look in the distance, and don't look at your phone. Giving people your undivided attention demonstrates your respect for them and establishes a strong connection, allowing empathy to flow between you.

Consider the reasons for another person's bad behavior before passing judgment. Is it because of bad experiences in the past, or because of personality traits over which they have no control?

Be selfless and considerate of others. Make sure your life includes an element of service in which you put the needs of others ahead of your own, such as caring for the sick or elderly, charity, or volunteer work. Altruism and service assist us in transcending separateness and connecting with others, resulting in an empathetic following.

Chapter 6

Developing Gratitude

Something about the Thanksgiving and Christmas seasons makes us feel grateful, or at least makes us believe we should. This piqued my interest in comparing and comprehending trends in selfishness over time. According to some studies, baby boomers are the most selfish generation, while others blame millennials for our entitled society. Social theorists may argue that selfish behavior is entirely dependent on the availability of human rights. There are numerous possible explanations.

Regardless, the literature is contradictory. You could argue and find evidence that the most heartless people are found in each decade. The truth is that selfishness is a human experience that occurs regardless of time or circumstance. It has always existed and will most likely continue to exist. Instead of focusing on who or what is to blame, why not direct our efforts toward altruistic solutions? Perhaps a gratitude practice? Gratitude is one of our most powerful tools for alleviating suffering. How is this accomplished?

The following are three techniques for increasing our gratitude. I propose that we remember them not just during the last two months of the year, but every day.

Be Wary
Suffering, according to Buddhist philosophy, is the result of selfishness. According to Christianity, we should seek the welfare of others rather than our own. Even those who do not have a religious or spiritual background are frustrated by the selfish behavior of others. Not only that but when we only focus on ourselves, we become lonely. Consider this: if you're the only one on your mind, do you have room to think about others? How can you cultivate relationships if you only live for yourself?

The truth is that the self is elusive. Why obsess over something as complex and ever-changing as our perceptions of ourselves? I'm not suggesting we think less of ourselves, but rather that we think less about ourselves. How are we going to accomplish this? Take note. I don't mean becoming more aware of who we think we are. This frequently serves only to feed the ego. I'm referring to raising our awareness of our own experience. This necessitates noticing and being curious about the present moment without passing judgment.

Be Open-Minded
Assume someone has stolen from you. "I would never do something like that," you might think, or "Of course, this happened to me, I must have a target on my back." Whether self-deprecating or self-inflating, thoughts like these aggravate our preconceived notions of the self and elicit feelings of anger and shame. Essentially, we are asking ourselves, "What does this experience say about me?" This doubt stems from a mind that still believes we are the most important, that we should be invincible, and that we should not have to suffer but only feel good. Because this way of thinking is unrealistic, there is another option: think differently. "This is disappointing," you may think, or "I wonder if those who stole were desperate?" You will most likely experience sadness, but you will recover emotionally faster. As a result, you may find peace in letting go. This time, the emphasis is on the present. It accepts reality and keeps our attention on what is rather than what is wrong or who is to blame. I recommend learning more about mindfulness and daily meditation to practice acceptance. And how can we shift our intentions away from the egoic self and toward compassion for others and our experience when we are not sitting cross-legged on the floor?

Be Understated
Much of our selfishness and suffering stems from our thoughts, not what we do or say. Our reality is greatly influenced by the thoughts we choose to focus on. Are your thoughts frequently filled with criticism and comparison? These are frequently formed when we attempt to exert control over others or our own experiences. Mind management necessitates deliberate work against cognitive distortions such as mind reading. Jumping to conclusions is a form of

mind reading. It happens when you believe you know what someone else is thinking. You define other people's motivations for doing what they do. This is done entirely on the basis of assumptions and, in most cases, with no physical evidence. We ignore other possibilities because our thoughts make sense to us and thus must be "true" or "valid."

When we are afraid and want to change the outcome, we frequently read people's minds. We want to change the situation because we are uncomfortable with it. It is selfish to refuse to allow others to think, do, and be as they wish. Assuming is anxiety caused by oneself. Now, don't judge yourself for falling into this habit: we all do it! Remember to be present in the moment and accept it for what it is.

How do we correct our distorted thinking now? Being unassuming, in essence, necessitates humility: a firm acknowledgment that we do not and cannot know everything. We expend a lot of energy believing that we need answers in order to feel good. What if the opposite was true? Perhaps we must choose to be okay in order to find solutions. So, how do we broaden our horizons? Consider the following:

Consider the following questions: Is there ever a time when this isn't true?" What perspectives should we consider when looking at it?" "Is this a useful thought?"Would I rather be correct or happy?"

Use gratitude statements to experiment with new ideas. For example, instead of thinking, "I'm a bad person," I could think, "I'm grateful for when I mess up." It's fantastic feedback for becoming the person I aspire to be!"

The brain is malleable. As a result, our behavior is as well. When we increase our awareness, accept reality, and stop assuming, we can think less about ourselves and more about others. Let us be grateful for our ability to think more about others and less about ourselves.

Chapter 7

The Art of Active Listening

In our interconnected world, mastering the art of listening is not only a valuable skill but also a foundational pillar of success. Those with the ability to listen stand out in a society that is often consumed by noise and distractions. These individuals forge deeper connections, exert influence, and foster harmonious relationships.

This chapter investigates the transformative power of effective listening. It delves into the profound effect that listening has on people's personal lives, professional endeavors, and overall well-being. By honing this fundamental skill, you can open doors and establish yourself as a respected individual in any field.

We waste universal time and cause pain when we fail or pretend to listen. It creates misunderstandings that did not need to exist in the first place. Yet, more often than we like to admit, all humans have committed the crime of failing to listen at some point in their lives.

The steps for Effective Listening are outlined below. Each is equally important. Each should be used in conjunction with the next. Listening takes time and practice, so be prepared to put in some effort.

Allow Others to Speak

It is all too common for the urge to interrupt and interject with our version of the story to arise during a conversation. This tendency reflects our ego's presence or our fear of forgetting our thoughts. However, when we deliberately silence ourselves and allow others to speak freely, we create a space in which invaluable wisdom and insights can emerge. Shutting up and embracing attentive silence allows for profound revelations that would otherwise be hidden.

If you feel the urge to interrupt, take a deep breath and consciously redirect your attention to listening more deeply. Pausing and tuning in to the speaker's words can sometimes reveal layers of understanding that go beyond our initial impulse to speak. Believe in the power of attentive listening and allow the other person to fully express themselves.

When trust is established in a conversation, both parties frequently develop nonverbal cues to indicate their willingness to contribute to the dialogue. These subtle body language skills can be used to indicate to the other person that you are ready to share your thoughts. Blinking at the same rate as the other person, for example, can convey engagement and receptivity. Using nonverbal cues, you can create a harmonious flow in which each participant feels respected and valued.

Develop Trust
There is an optimal space where energy flows freely within the realm of conversation. This environment fosters a sense of ease and openness for both participants. When a sacred ground is built on trust, it becomes fertile soil for profound insights and authentic connections to flourish. Trust allows for vulnerability and the discovery of hidden talents, but it is not given freely; it must be earned by both parties involved.

It is critical to invest the necessary time and effort in cultivating trust. Remembering and demonstrating sincere concern, such as recalling important details shared in previous conversations (e.g., an approaching birthday and asking about plans), helps to build trust. Being inclusive and actively participating in dialogue by asking thoughtful questions builds trust and inclusivity.

Furthermore, the willingness to overcome preconceived notions, add value, and maintain credibility in your interactions contributes to trust. Confidentiality is also essential; if asked to keep something confidential, it must be kept confidential. Such actions reinforce the importance of respecting boundaries.

Navigating a delicate balance of various elements is what active listening entails. It entails listening to and comprehending what is said, observing body language for deeper understanding, tapping into the energy created by the exchange, and cultivating a sense of comfort that encourages both individuals to support each other's progress. This encouraging environment includes a willingness to give and receive constructive feedback, promoting mutual growth and development.

Conversations exceed superficiality and pave the way for authentic connections and transformative insights within this sacred space of trust, nurtured over time and genuine engagement.

Language Understanding
Effective communication in any conversation extends beyond the mere exchange of words between individuals. The majority of communication occurs through nonverbal cues such as body language, vocal tone, pacing, and even the silence that pervades the conversation. These silent intervals have enormous power, allowing both participants to delve deeper into their thoughts and creating an environment in which unspoken words can be heard.

A skilled listener fosters an environment conducive to open dialogue. Begin by being aware of your body language. Make sure it conveys openness and receptivity. A warm smile and deep breaths can set the tone for expressive freedom.

It's worth noting that women prefer direct eye contact, whereas men may prefer a mix of direct and indirect eye contact depending on the situation. Remember to relax and avoid crossing your arms, as these gestures may be misinterpreted as defensiveness or disinterest. Maintain a neutral facial expression while paying close attention to your responses to the conversation.

If you're interested in this subject, look into the nuances of nonverbal cues like facial expressions, gestures, and tone of voice. Recognizing and respecting cultural differences in communication styles and norms can also improve cross-cultural listening, ensure inclusivity, and avoid misunderstandings. Comprehensive knowledge leads to comprehension.

Nonverbal cues go beyond body language; breathing synchronization can also help to establish trust and rapport. Aligning your breathing can help you feel more connected and empathic. Furthermore, you can use your breathing patterns to guide the person into a different emotional state. For example, if they are upset and breathing rapidly, taking slow and deep breaths yourself can help them naturally shift their emotional state.

Having Insight

It is not uncommon to have intuitive nudges or gut feelings during a conversation that invite us to a deeper level of connection. These nuances and signals should never be overlooked. They frequently hold the key to eliciting profound insights and facilitating meaningful dialogue. Trusting your intuition allows you to speak up and share these valuable insights, enriching the conversation with new perspectives and dimensions.

If you are experiencing intuitive prompting, even if it appears unusual, it is critical that you trust yourself and give voice to your thoughts. You can start by saying something like, "I know this sounds strange, but I have a strong gut feeling I believe is worth sharing." 'Are you willing to listen?' You can also acknowledge the possibility of error by saying, 'I could be wrong about this, but...' When you express your intuition with humility and openness, you create an environment in which new ideas and insights can emerge.

By utilizing the power of intuition in your conversations, you cultivate confidence in both yourself and the dialogue. Expect the conversation to flow with inspiration and genuine interest as you pay close attention to your intuitive cues. These heart-led exchanges transcend the limitations of words and find peace in silence. Through intuitive listening, you can access a level of understanding that goes beyond the surface, allowing profound connections and transformative conversations to emerge.

Making Notations

Taking notes during a conversation can help you focus and retain important information for future reference. Taking notes allows you to capture the fundamentals of the conversation and provides an exact record of the key points discussed.

Recognize, however, that note-taking may have different effects on different people. Writing can help some people process and internalize spoken words, as well as deepen their understanding. On the other hand, it may serve as a distraction.

It is beneficial to experiment and discover a method that works best for you when it comes to note-taking. Experiment with different techniques until you find a happy medium between actively participating in the conversation and capturing key points in your notes. This way, you can reap the benefits of taking notes while remaining fully present and attentive to the ongoing conversation.

Develop a shorthand system that allows you to quickly record ideas without disrupting the flow of the conversation. This method allows you to take notes while reducing the time and effort required for extensive note-taking. Consider using symbols or abbreviations with personal meaning as memory triggers when reviewing your notes later on.

Empathy Formation

Empathy and listening are inextricably linked and serve as the foundation for meaningful and impactful communication. We transcend hearing and enter a realm of understanding and connection when we listen with empathy.

When we tune in to our emotions, experiences, and perspectives, we create a safe space for genuine expression. This builds trust, encourages open dialogue, and strengthens bonds. Listening with empathy demonstrates compassion, validation, and a desire to understand others. We create a more compassionate and understanding society by putting ourselves in their shoes.

Effective listening ensures that everyone understands what is being said. Active listening techniques such as paraphrasing, reflecting, and asking open-ended questions are used. These techniques improve listening skills, show genuine interest in the speaker's message, and promote comprehension.

Within the conversation, repeating and clarifying information helps to confirm mutual interpretation. Using explanation phrases like the ones below helps with clarification and alignment.

★ *So, what am I hearing you say...*
★ *Could you please explain that to me again?*
★ *What do you mean...?*
★ *What do you think about...?*
★ *What are your thoughts on...?*
★ *What are your suggestions?*

This step has the potential for boredom, awkwardness, and repetition, but it is necessary for genuine comprehension and alignment. Before concluding, create an explanation or summary of the conversation to eliminate presumptions. When you recap the key points and actions, shared understanding and accountability are established. This is also the time to confirm future actions, ensuring follow-through.

Insisting on explanations and summaries does not constitute an attempt to disrupt or bully. It serves as a reminder of the value of active listening. Time is saved, misunderstandings are reduced, and mutual comprehension is prioritized by reiterating and summarizing the discussion.

Effective listening has the potential to transform our interactions, relationships, and personal development. We can cultivate profound connections, foster trust, and uncover hidden insights by embracing the principles of attentive listening. We've looked at different aspects of authoritative listening, realizing that authority comes from creating spaces for meaningful dialogue rather than dominating conversations.

Furthermore, we have discussed the importance of patience, taking notes, and the art of summarizing in order to solidify comprehension and foster accountability. We empower ourselves to become authoritative listeners capable of influencing outcomes, fostering empathy, and inspiring growth by incorporating these practices into our conversations.

Chapter 8

Finding Meaning in Generosity

Joy or happiness is a mental state. It is a sensation that helps people stay healthy and fit. There is a well-known saying that goes, 'The more you give of yourself, the more you find yourself.' Giving is important for a variety of reasons. It is a way to express gratitude, say thank you, or show someone you care. It can be difficult to express true feelings in words at times, but giving a token of appreciation not only represents your feelings but also lets the recipient know how much you appreciate them. Many people we encounter in our daily lives may make our lives easier, such as neighbors, coworkers, or even mail carriers or the local grocery store cashier. While giving does not always have to be in the form of a gift, saying thank you with a kind word or a friendly smile goes a long way toward encouraging the chances of a friendly and successful relationship.

Giving food to the needy, household items to a family whose home may have burned down, and even monetary donations to a children's charity can make a significant difference. Giving is an important characteristic to instill in children. For example, if a child assists in selecting a gift for a family member who is celebrating a birthday and then presents that gift to them, it teaches them to be selfless, to share, and to appreciate the pleasure of giving to others. Teaching by example is the most effective way to teach a child how to give not only gifts but also in other ways. Visiting someone in the hospital, sending a thank you, get well, or congratulations card, and even sending Christmas cards are all wonderful ways to teach a child the value of giving. Giving can take the form of time, gifts, cards, or kind words. A manager who gives his employees time off, bonuses, or other incentives for a job well done will undoubtedly reap the benefits of giving. Giving is all about receiving; that is, the more you give, the more you receive.

It is a hidden barter in which we give something we have in exchange for happiness without asking for it. When we give something, however, we should not expect anything in return. Give with all of one's heart and then forget about it. The irony is that we are happiest when we give without selfish motives. The dictionary defines giving as the voluntary transfer of property without receiving anything in return. Giving and assisting others is something that everyone should do. Generosity is simply the habit of giving. People who are generous and believe in the joy of giving are blessed. It is unquestionably a charitable act that spreads happiness and peace and allows goodness to prevail in the world!

There are times in our lives when we begin to understand the true meaning of life and its impact on others. The 'joy of giving' is one such feeling. At times, we realize that gaining or acquiring some 'gain' provides less pleasure than 'parting with it and giving it to a destitute/someone who is truly in need'. It provides immense pleasure that can only be experienced and is difficult to explain. And the good news is that sharing is never a waste of time. It is also a harsh reality that the 'pursuit of attaining something in excess' leads nowhere and ultimately causes stress. It is not only about money or wealth when people share. Generosity is only one of many factors. It is about being kind, helpful, selfless, sacrificing, giving, serving, loving, and so on. Also, a few words of sympathy can go a long way.

There is a certain satisfaction in receiving something. That is the joy that children feel when they receive items such as toffees and toys. Giving makes parents and grandparents happy. The joy of giving is far greater than the joy of receiving.

When we see a good movie, for example, we tell everyone about it, even if we don't think they should see it. The filmmaker is not paying us a fee to do this! We simply believe that our loved ones should have the same opportunity. For example, an elderly lady who prepares various dishes for her grandchildren finds great joy in doing so. People who give report higher levels of happiness than those who receive. Gradually shifting from a taking to a giving mindset cleanses the mind and brings immense joy.

Winston Churchill once said, "We make a living by what we get." What we give defines our lives."We can never be depressed if we consider how we can help those around us. People who are depressed are unaware of this. They become depressed because they only think about themselves. They will notice that their depression has lifted once they begin to give or serve.

We should take advantage of any opportunity to be useful. If we are uncomfortable despite our meditation and other practices, we should do something to bring happiness and comfort to others. Giving is necessary for spiritual development.

Serving in any way we can, whether by donating our time, and money or simply speaking about positive things, raises our consciousness. "How can we be useful to the people around us, and to the entire world?" Then our hearts begin to bloom.

One aspect of caring and sharing is charitable giving. Nonetheless, we can do it individually in a variety of ways while celebrating the joy of giving. When we share something, we connect with others in a variety of ways. It's a divine quality. Giving can make a difference in the lives of others, giving us a sense of empowerment, pride, and accomplishment.

Conclusion

It probably won't surprise you to learn that acting unselfishly is the best way to overcome selfishness. Sounds easy, doesn't it? However, simply knowing how not to be is insufficient.

The goal here is to exchange something that has benefited you in some way for something that will benefit others more and you more in the long run. You're not going to stick with it unless you see it that way. It goes without saying that some of these will be more difficult for you than others. Here's a synopsis of the entire chapter:

Make contact
When was the last time you called or texted a family member or a friend? Or when was the last time you had a heart-to-heart with someone about something important to both of you?

Check in on them if it's been a while, invite them over for tea/coffee and something, or check to see if they require anything. If there is a lot of snow on the ground, inquire if they require assistance with shoveling. If they're sick, ask if you can pick up some items for them at the store.

Make their lives easier or more enjoyable for them. Most of the time, it will make the day more memorable for you as well.

Inquire about other people's days
And pay attention long enough to get the full (unpolite) answer. "Fine." is the most common response. "You?" or something along those lines. They figure that's the answer most people want to hear. But if you suspect they're only saying that to appear brave, there's no harm in gently pressing with something like, "Is there anything I can do to make your day better?" or "What would make your day better?" Then listen carefully to what the individual has to say.

Listening intently

Give the speaker your full attention, and be sure to listen to understand rather than just respond. Concentrate on making them feel heard and understood, and remind yourself that you would expect the same if you were trying to communicate with someone else.

Consider the following guidelines for practicing active listening:

- ★ *Make eye contact.*
- ★ *Allow the other person to speak without interfering or responding.*
- ★ *Display encouraging and attentive body language.*
- ★ *Summarize or rephrase what they're saying.*

In order to better understand what they're saying, ask pertinent questions. Helping them feel heard takes precedence over arguing your own point.

Sometimes put others' needs before yours

I'm not talking about situations where you're on an airplane with your kids and the masks fall off. Which mask do you wear first?" Consider a situation in which your desires clashed with the needs of another person.

- ★ *You want to smoke, but there is someone in the room who has asthma.*
- ★ *You want to listen to your favorite music, but your roommate is sleeping.*

Putting the needs of others first is sometimes the only option. However, it is also necessary to distinguish between wants and needs.

For example, suppose you don't want to be a parent but your partner can't wait to be one. It's sometimes better to be open and honest about what you want and why.

Everyone is experiencing something

Don't make the mistake of assuming that someone else's path is easier, or that their load is lighter than yours.

You have no idea what's going on behind the scenes of other people's lives. Unless you're close to them, you probably don't get to hear about what's really going on with them — what they're going through or why they share certain things but not others.

It's far too easy to presume they're simply lazy or too self-centered to consider the needs of those around them if you don't know that.

Instead of passing judgment on what you see, simply let them know you're available if they ever need a friendly ear. Otherwise, you'd be better off ignoring each other.

Perform frequent self-checks

It can help to ask yourself, "What have I done for someone else today?"

If you are aware that you are prone to selfish behavior, it is a good idea to conduct regular self-checks. Make it a habit to plan on doing something helpful or thoughtful for someone every morning, without advertising it or expecting praise or gratitude.

When you disagree with someone, ask yourself the following questions:

- ★ *"Am I being impolite or impolite?"*
- ★ *"Is it possible that I'm making assumptions about this person?"*
- ★ *"What could I do to help us both get through this?"*

Not every squabble between you and others will be your fault. However, be prepared to confront yourself with difficult questions when others become angry with you.

Your thoughts

Yours isn't the only one that counts. Allow others the time and space to express themselves without being critical or judgmental. When you show your cards and it's clear that you're more concerned with being right and shaming someone for thinking differently, your welcome tends to expire.

On a related note, it's tempting to respond harshly and put the other person in their place when you're the target of judgment or rude behavior.

But, unless speaking up will actually help someone other than yourself, it's best to just give the jerk a pass and let them go.

Stay in the present moment
Create a new habit of mindfulness meditation and cultivate the ability to center yourself when things become chaotic. Download a meditation or mindfulness app to assist you in developing this habit and incorporating it into your daily routine.

Every morning should begin with a few minutes of meditation. It's a new day, and being aware of the present moment allows you to live it consciously, allowing you to make better decisions and communicate with loved ones more mindfully. Obsessing over the past or worrying about the future makes it more difficult to avoid behaving selfishly toward others. Other people aren't present for you if you're not in the present.

Practice gratitude on a regular basis
Make it a daily priority to identify three things you're grateful for every morning and before bedtime. You can write them down or say them aloud, but your gratitude will be more powerful in your brain if you include your body as well as your thoughts.
Consider the following suggestions for making gratitude a daily priority:

 ★ *Make gratitude statements a regular part of your journaling or planning page.*

 ★ *Collect gratitude affirmations and begin each day with one of your favorites.*

★ *Put gratitude affirmations or reminders in places where you will see them.*

★ *Set reminders to remind you to express gratitude for something.*

Determine what other people bring to the table.
Others have good ideas as well. Other members of your team may have untapped talents or gifts. Not all of those skills will be useful, but each member has something to offer.

The more you get to know your coworkers or colleagues, the easier it will be to see where they will shine. By assisting them in doing so, you can make their work more enjoyable for them and their results more profitable for your employer. Everyone is good at something that can help the world.

Give your time to help others
Find opportunities to serve those you've grown accustomed to viewing as an alien species. You understand what I mean. To some extent, we all engage in selective empathy.

However, putting yourself out there and volunteering your time and energy to help those with whom you do not normally identify can broaden your perspective and change the way you interact with others. It has the potential to transform your life and make you a better person. So, aside from your preconceived notions, what do you really stand to lose?

Donate
Find organizations that do important work for you and support them with your hard-earned money. If you want to start small, or if you don't have much money right now, look for ethically sourced or ethically made products to support you.

It's simple to find products made by underserved communities. And, while they may be more expensive than what you can get at

Walmart, you'll know that the money you spend on handcrafted items will benefit real people in difficult situations. When you look at it, you'll notice a person who appreciates that you prioritized their goods over short-term savings.

Those in dare need
Set aside a portion of your income for random gifts. These can be small, frequent gifts or larger, infrequent gifts. The main criterion for this type of giving is that you do not expect to be reimbursed. The money has vanished. You're releasing it to the universe as a thank-you for all the blessings you've received. You're paying it forward without expecting to be recognized, thanked, or rewarded.

Which of the above tips will you put into practice this week to overcome selfishness in a relationship? Which will you tackle first? If you're an introvert, the more socially demanding strategies will be more difficult to adopt, let alone incorporate into your daily routine. But try to pick at least one of them to put yourself to the test. You will not be sorry for becoming more present for the people who are important to you.

Made in the USA
Las Vegas, NV
10 December 2024

13813123R00030